I0810921

Life Cycles of Living Things

Bird Life Cycle

Tracy Vonder Brink

Table of Contents

Bird Life Cycle 3
Words to Know 22
Index. 23
Comprehension Questions 23
About the Author 24

A Starfish Book

SEAHORSE PUBLISHING

Teaching Tips for Caregivers:

As a caregiver, you can help your child succeed in school by giving them a strong foundation in language and literacy skills and a desire to learn to read.

This book helps children grow by letting them practice reading skills.

Reading for pleasure and interest will help your child to develop reading skills and will give your child the opportunity to practice these skills in meaningful ways.

- Encourage your child to read on her own at home
- Encourage your child to practice reading aloud
- Encourage activities that require reading
- Establish a reading time
- Talk with your child
- Give your child writing materials

Teaching Tips for Teachers:

Research shows that one of the best ways for students to learn a new topic is to read about it.

Before Reading

- Read the "Words to Know" and discuss the meaning of each word.
- Read the back cover to see what the book is about.

During Reading

- When a student gets to a word that is unknown, ask them to look at the rest of the sentence to find clues to help with the meaning of the unknown word.
- Ask the student to write down any pages of the book that were confusing to them.

After Reading

- Discuss the main idea of the book.
- Ask students to give one detail that they learned in the book by showing a text dependent answer from the book.

Bird Life Cycle

All living things are born.

They grow to be adults.

We call these changes a life cycle.

Birds are animals with backbones.

They have feathers and wings.

Birds are **warm-blooded**.

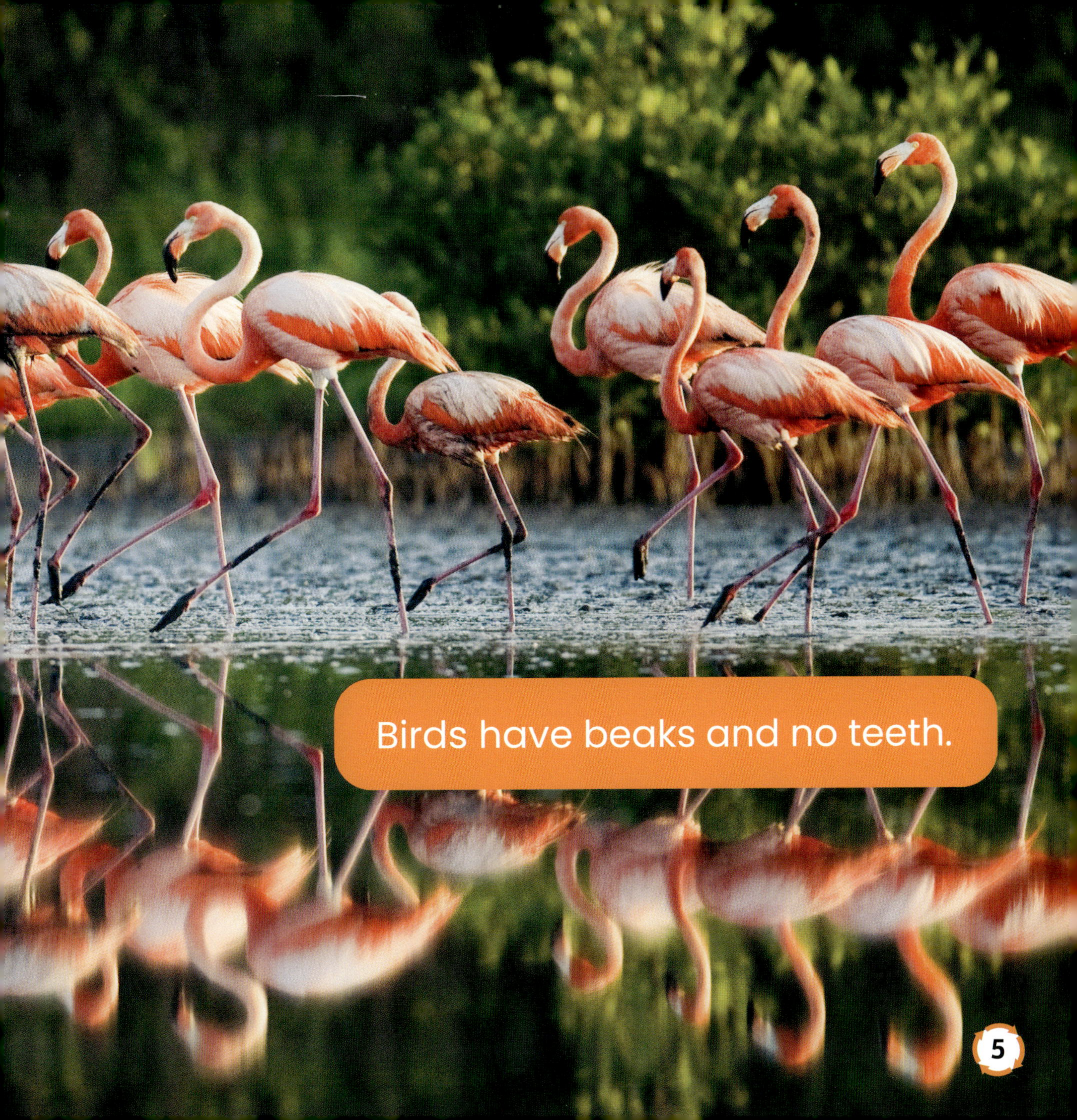

Birds have beaks and no teeth.

A bird's life cycle begins with an egg.

An **embryo** grows inside.

The egg must be kept warm.

A parent sits on it.

Sometimes, the male and female take turns sitting on the egg.

A penguin holds its egg on its feet to keep it off the cold ground.

A **hatchling** breaks out of its egg.

The hatchling has no feathers. Its eyes may be closed.

The hatchling grows into a **nestling**.

It stays in the nest.

Its parents feed it and keep it warm.

Many birds feed insects to their nestlings.

The nestling becomes a **fledgling**.

It grows feathers and learns to fly.

Its parents may still care for it.

An **immature** bird lives on its own.

It looks like a grown bird.

But it cannot yet have its own babies.

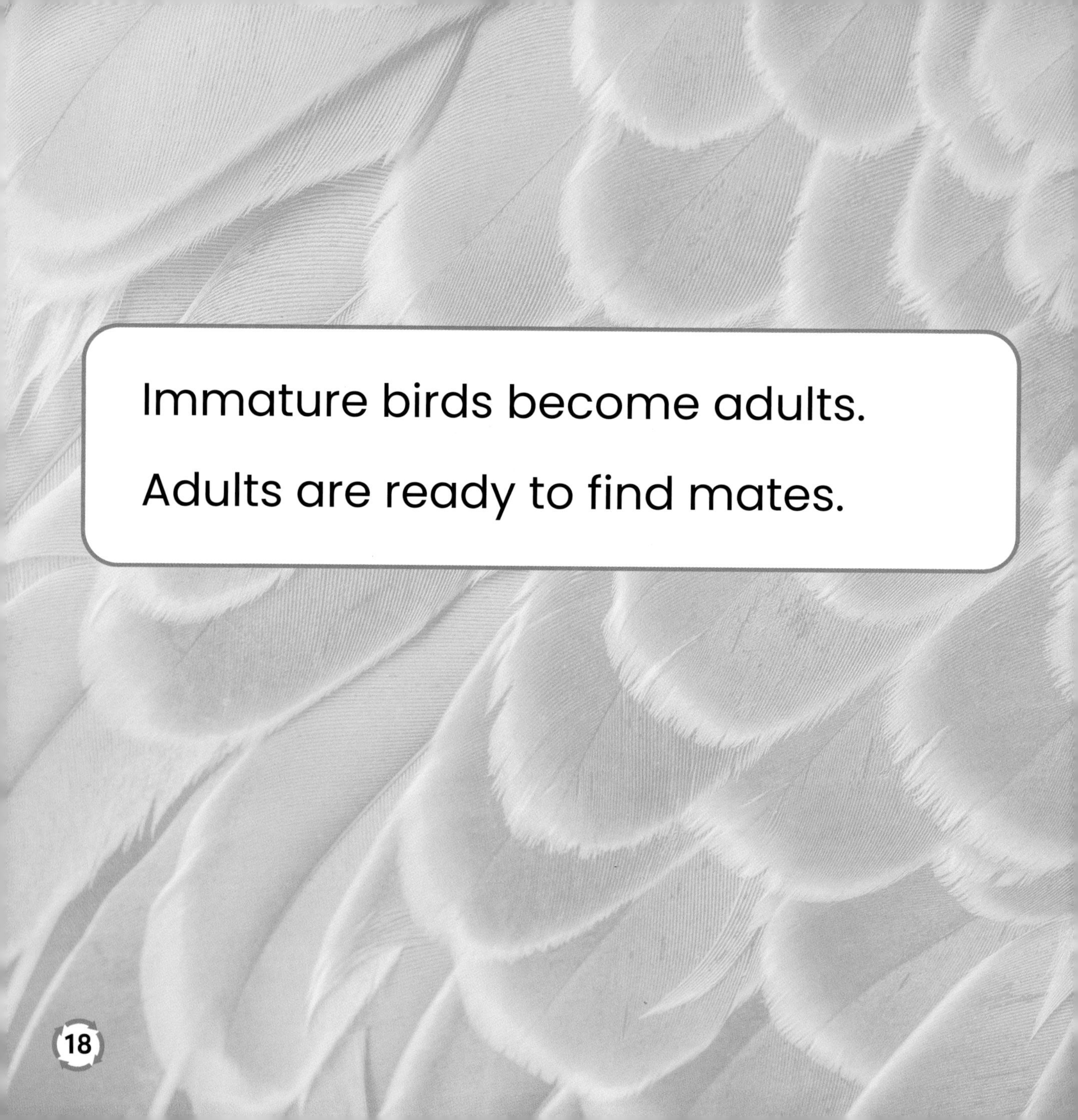

Immature birds become adults.

Adults are ready to find mates.

Some birds, such as swans, keep the same mate for life.

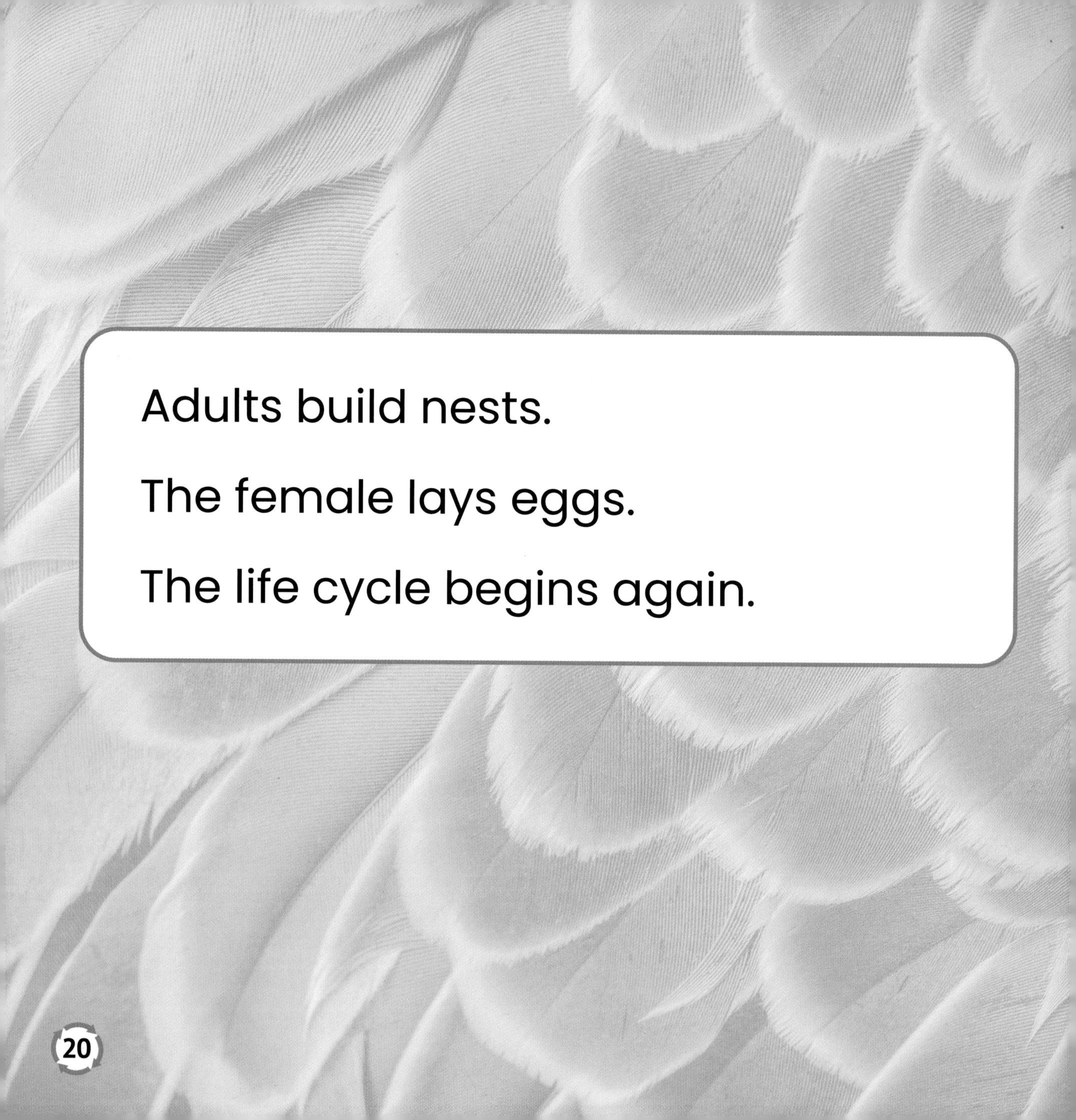

Adults build nests.

The female lays eggs.

The life cycle begins again.

Words to Know

embryo (EM-bree-oh): a living creature in the earliest stage of development, before it is hatched or born

fledgling (FLEJ-ling): a young bird that has grown feathers and is learning to fly

hatchling (HACH-ling): a young animal that has newly hatched from an egg

immature (im-uh-CHOOR): not fully grown or developed

nestling (NEST-ling): a young bird that has not left the nest

warm-blooded (worm BLUHD-id): able to make body heat; having a warm body temperature that does not change even if the surrounding temperature is very hot or very cold

Index

egg(s) 6, 8, 9, 11, 20
feathers 4, 11, 15
fledgling 15
hatchling 11, 12
immature 17, 18
nestling 12, 13, 15

Comprehension Questions

1. A bird's life cycle begins with
   a. a nestling. **b.** a hatchling. **c.** an egg.
2. A young bird that has grown feathers is called
   a. a fledgling.
   b. a hatchling.
   c. a nestling.
3. An immature bird
   a. lives on its own.
   b. stays in the nest.
   c. is taken care of by its parents.
4. **True or false:** An immature bird can have its own babies.
5. **True or false:** Adult birds build nests.

Answers
1. c 2. a 3. a 4. False 5. True

About the Author

Tracy Vonder Brink loves true stories and facts. She has written more than twenty books for kids and is a contributing editor for three children's science magazines. Tracy lives in Cincinnati, Ohio, with her husband, two daughters, and two rescue dogs.

Written by: Tracy Vonder Brink
Design by: Bobbie Houser
Editor: Kim Thompson

Photographs:
t = Top, b = Bottom, c = Center, l = Left, r = Right

Shutterstock: starryvoyage: cover tl; Reimar: cover tr; collin meloche: cover b; palex1977: p. 3 l; Wendy Rentz p. 3 cl; Randall Vermillion: p. 3 cr; Calin Tatu: p. 3 r; GUDKOV ANDREY: pp. 4-5; Vishnevskiy Vasily: p. 7; Brandon B: p. 9; Gabrielle Hovey: p. 10; PCHT: p. 13; Bachkova Natalia: pp. 14-15; jaboticaba images: p. 16; Dark_Side: p. 19; Angela N Perryman: p. 21

Library of Congress PCN Data
Bird Life Cycle / Tracy Vonder Brink
Life Cycles of Living Things
ISBN 978-1-63897-452-9 (hard cover)
ISBN 978-1-63897-567-0 (paperback)
ISBN 978-1-63897-682-0 (EPUB)
ISBN 978-1-63897-797-1 (eBook)
Library of Congress Control Number: 2021953380

Printed in the United States of America.

Seahorse Publishing Company
www.seahorsepub.com

Published in the United States
Seahorse Publishing
PO Box 771325
Coral Springs, FL 33077

SEAHORSE PUBLISHING